T.

John Gunstone has been a parish priest in the Church of England, Chaplain of the former Barnabas Fellowship at Whatcombe House in Dorset, and County Ecumenical Officer in Greater Manchester. He has written a number of books, including *Healed, Restored, Forgiven: Liturgies, Prayers and Readings for the Ministry of Healing* and *A Touching Place: The Ministry of Healing in the Local Church: A Practical Handbook*, both published by Canterbury Press. He is a Canon Emeritus of Manchester Cathedral.

Take Heart

Healing prayer for the whole of life

John Gunstone

CANTERBURY
PRESS
Norwich

© John Gunstone 2006

First published in 2006 by the Canterbury Press Norwich
(a publishing imprint of Hymns Ancient & Modern Limited,
a registered charity)
9–17 St Alban's Place, London N1 0NX

www.scm-canterburypress.co.uk

British Library Cataloguing in Publication data

A catalogue record for this book is available
from the British Library

ISBN 1-85311-739-0/978-1-85311-739-8

Typeset by Regent Typesetting, London
Printed and bound by
Bookmarque, Croydon, Surrey

Contents

Jesus stood still and said, 'Call him here.' And they called the blind man, saying to him, 'Take heart; get up, he is calling you.'

Mark 10.49

Introduction

Most of us, I imagine, have little difficulty in praying when we're feeling contented or thankful; but prayer can be more of a problem when we're sorrowful or angry. This book attempts to illustrate how we can pray through the latter state as well as the former. I have written it in the belief that, since feelings are intimately interwoven with the human nature God created, they can be transfigured into an act of obedience to the Father through our union with Jesus Christ in the power of his Spirit.

I have selected twelve out of the many feelings we experience as examples of how to pray through them. There is, of course, much overlap in our emotions, and we can slide from one to the other. So, for example, I have not written about praying through a depression, though I have referred to it in connection with other feelings I have included.

Each chapter has four sections: Reflections, Reading, Scriptures and Prayer.

Reflections

These are not intended to be psychological notes, ethical comments or theological essays. They are simply the kind of ideas, questions and memories which may come into our minds while we are experiencing an emotion, or afterwards when we are able to reflect on it.

Reading

These are a random selection of brief quotations taken from books I have read in recent years. Some refer directly, others obliquely to the subject. Each represents the comment a friend might make after they have listened to what we have told them about our feelings. Often it is just one thing they have said which we remember, because at the time it was so helpful.

Scriptures

Armed, as it were, with some understanding of our emotions, and with a wise word from a friend, we turn to the Bible. If we are regular scripture readers, we will from time to time come across a verse or a passage which seems to speak to us about what we are feeling. For this section I have chosen three short pieces: one from the Psalms (the Psalmist is for me the most helpful scribe in the Old Testament where our emotions are concerned), another from the apostolic letters, and the last from the Gospels.

Prayer

The final section is a prayer in response to our feelings, our thoughts, the words of others, and the scripture passages. Obviously these prayers are very personal; they reflect my own experiences of 'emotion recollected in tranquillity'. But I hope they may serve as imperfect models to help readers to do something similar when the need arises.

We cannot expect our wayward feelings to be transfigured through one prayer. We may need to pray through them again and again. But, hopefully, in the grace of God, we shall eventually discover that we are learning to turn to him more readily as these emotions arise, and when they do they become incentives for confession, intercession and praise.

I should add that this book does not attempt to discuss the deeper and wider implications of our feelings and our reactions to them. In certain circumstances individuals may need the help of a trained counsellor or a medical adviser. But such professional help does not bypass the need for prayer; indeed, it makes such prayer all the more necessary.

I

Belonging

Reflections

If someone asks who I am, I reply by giving my surname as well as my Christian name. My Christian name identifies me as an individual for whom Jesus died (which 'forename' does not); my surname shows that I am a member of a particular family.

That surname reminds me how much I owe to my ancestors. Physical appearance and gestures, together with much else about me, can be traced back to my parents, to my grandparents, and back beyond them through countless generations. When news of the genome was publicized years ago, a Christian physicist is reported to have said, 'Now we know the tools God used to create us.'

A cousin of mine served in the Second World War as a fitter in the Fleet Air Arm. Many years later he visited the Arm's museum at Yeovil and spent a long time in the exhibition hall gazing at a Fairey Barracuda torpedo-bomber suspended from the roof. When his wife urged him to move on, it was as if he came out of a dream, and he said, 'I once knew every rivet and wire in that aircraft.'

And so God knows us – more intimately than we know ourselves. Our deep consciousness, our buried memories and our hidden fears – nothing is hidden from him. In the words of the Psalmist, he knows our 'inward parts' (139.13): our bodies and everything about us which makes each one of us a unique personality. This verse comes in the midst of a song which is full of wonder that God, who is the Creator of the universe, has known us as individuals from the moment we were conceived in our mother's womb.

Knowledge of our ancestry contributes to our sense of belonging. We look back on our family tree with its Christian names and surnames, back into the last century and beyond, and we feel we are learning a little more about ourselves. As our society becomes more fragmented and scattered, tracing one's family tree has become a major interest for many people. It helps them to know themselves.

The BBC2 series *Who Do You Think You Are?* arranged for a number of well-known personalities to trace their forebears back several generations through visits to places associated with them, followed up by searches among registers and other documents in the archives departments. On the screen their faces showed they were deeply moved by what they learned. Some of their ancestors had been exceptionally resourceful in the face of suffering and injustice. At the end of their programme, they nearly all affirmed that their understanding of themselves had changed.

I felt as they did when I saw the signatures of my parents (now dead) in the register of the church where they were married, or when I visited the graves of relatives in churchyards in Derbyshire and Somerset. It was easy to turn that feeling of belonging into a prayer of thankfulness to God, both for them and for what they had handed on to me now.

But besides surnames we have Christian names, given to us when we were christened. It was Pope John XXIII who said that the most important thing in his life was not that he had been ordained a priest and a bishop, nor that he had been elected Pope, but that he had been baptized.

Baptism is important because through this sacrament and all that it involves we are reborn into a new life. We are forgiven for what in the past has separated us from God and, through Jesus' death and resurrection, we become united with Christ in his family, the redeemed community. And this, the greatest of privileges, is not through any ancestral inheritance or personal worth, but through God's grace, who adopts us as his children. We become heirs to his kingdom.

Occasionally I have been privileged to attend the baptism of students and others from countries where being a Christian is far from easy. As these young men and women have come to a font, or stepped out of a baptismal pool, I have felt humbled by their faith and courage as I realized what it was going to mean for them. They were being received by God into a radically different lifestyle from the majority of those to whom they were returning when their visit to Britain ended. Back home they would be at risk of being ostracized, of having their churches and homes vandalized, and perhaps of being imprisoned.

Our sense of belonging to God's family is strengthened by our worship and fellowship with other Christians. This is what upholds the faith of those who seek to follow Christ in the kind of countries I have just mentioned. This is why so often we have a warm feeling of acceptance renewed in us when we've been to church. But sometimes it isn't always like that. There are occasions when our feelings are very different – when we felt the worship was cold, and fellow members of the congregation were uninterested in us. Christians don't always express that loving acceptance which is expected of us. That is why we often give the impression to visitors and outsiders that we are no more faithful to our beliefs than the members of a temperance society would if they were frequently drunk!

We need to recall that when we were baptized we began a spiritual journey, and on that journey we are all at different stages. There are times when the pilgrimage is joyful and companionable; there are other times when our faith is cool and our attitude towards others is cool, too. The repentance to which we were formally summoned in the baptism service has to be renewed every day. Belonging to the Church is not founded on the feelings about worship, or about our relationships with other members, but on what God has done for us in Christ.

When we enjoy feelings of belonging, then, it becomes easy to direct our praises to God, both as our Creator (through whom we got our surname) and as our Redeemer (who gave us our Christian name). Then we want to let our prayer of thanksgiving ripple out in widening circles to our natural family, our friends, our colleagues, our neighbourhood, our country, and the human family.

And with our thanksgivings go our intercessions and responsibilities as Christians for those in these widening circles.

Reading

Although baptism is a decisive moment, when a human life is orientated in one direction rather than another, and although it is complete in itself, gathering up all the riches of Christian initiation, it is at the same time a beginning, the point of entry into Christianity. Even an adult does not issue from his or her baptism already a complete Christian. There is still much to learn, new repentances to be made, services to be undertaken, new occasions for receiving the Spirit of God . . . But perhaps the important point is that the process has already begun; the decisive event *has* taken place.

John Macquarrie

Scriptures

It was you who formed my inward parts;
    you knit me together in my mother's womb.
I praise you, for I am fearfully and wonderfully made.
    Wonderful are your works;
that I know very well.
    My frame was not hidden from you,
when I was being made in secret,
    intricately woven in the depths of the earth.
Your eyes beheld my unformed substance.
In your book were written
    all the days that were formed for me,
    when none of them as yet existed.

Psalm 139.13–16

When the goodness and loving-kindness of God our Saviour appeared, he saved us, not because of any works of righteousness that we had done, but according to his mercy, through the water of rebirth and renewal by the Holy Spirit. This Spirit he poured out on us richly through Jesus Christ our Saviour, so that, having been justified by his grace, we might become heirs according to the hope of eternal life.

Titus 3.4–7

John the baptizer proclaimed, 'The one who is more powerful than I is coming after me; I am not worthy to stoop down and untie the thong of his sandals. I have baptized you with water; but he will baptize you with the Holy Spirit.' In those days Jesus came from Nazareth of Galilee and was baptized by John in the Jordan. And just as he was coming up out

of the water, he saw the heavens torn apart and the Spirit
descending like a dove on him. And a voice came from heaven,
'You are my Son, the Beloved; with you I am well pleased.'

Mark 1.7–11

Prayer

I praise and thank you, heavenly Father,
that in the midst of the vastness of your creation
you made me, conceived through my natural father
and carried in the womb of my mother.

Through those nine months
the genetic story of their parents and families
shaped me secretly as the next chapter in that story,
to be born in your image and to live for your love.

Help me, Lord, to accept myself as I am,
and teach me to love myself, not for myself,
nor just for what I am in the story of my family,
but because of what I am by grace in your sight.

Take the thankfulness I feel for my parents
and for all those with whom I am joined
in the human family,
and consecrate it when I next share with your family
in the eucharist of Christ's Body and Blood.

But above all I pray that I may never lose
that sense of thankfulness springing from the truth
that you have sent your Son to redeem me,
and to encourage me to grow into his image
through the power of the Holy Spirit.

2

Doubt

Reflections

In this modern culture where we are mentally programmed to question everything, it is not surprising that we find our faith challenged from time to time. Fresh discoveries about the created universe, with its unimaginable greatness on one hand and its inconceivable sub-atomic smallness on the other, send our minds in a whirl as we wonder how God could have created it.

Then the appalling sufferings which affect nations, ethnic groups, families and individuals every day, vividly presented to us by the media, seem to mock the Gospel proclamation that God is a God of love. Tragedies, accidents and illnesses which distress those dearest to us open up chasms of doubt. It can be the same when we are afflicted ourselves.

Recently, two people I know had cancer. One was a young woman who was diagnosed with the disease while she was at school, but in spite of this she bravely fulfilled her ambition to be a teacher, though her time at university was interrupted by weeks in hospital. She became a much-loved teacher in a primary school. Her happiness was crowned when she married. But a year or so after the wedding, she suddenly died. She was only twenty-eight.

The other is a slightly older man, also a teacher. He was warned he only had one or two months to live, but the hospital continued to treat him and, as the months went by, his condition gradually improved. Then, in the same week that the young woman died, he underwent various scans and was told that the signs of the cancer had disappeared.

And so it was that I found myself in the almost unbearable tension of simultaneously 'rejoicing with those who rejoice and weeping with those who weep'. But still the question nagged: 'Where was the Lord's justice in this?' Both were faithful Christians. Both were the focus of much prayer. Had God forgotten to be gracious to the young woman?

Perhaps we hesitate to voice our doubts for fear of what our believing friends might think. Would they sadly conclude that we were losing our faith if we shared our questions with them? A sense of guilt chills us. Singing hymns in church boldly asserting that Jesus is Lord of all increases our discomfort.

Yet the Psalmist was not afraid to express his feelings of doubt when he spoke to God. He wanted to know why it was that the wicked prospered and were not punished for their sin (Psalm 73.3). He cried out in anguish when his enemies oppressed him (Psalm 42.9). And he composed the prayer which Jesus invoked in his agony on the cross: 'My God, my God, why have you forsaken me?' (Psalm 22.1).

If the humanity of Jesus, though mysteriously united with the Godhead, could pray such a question at the most critical moment of his life, then surely we, in the weakness of our frail humanity, are not being faithless when we cry out to God as we struggle with our doubts?

We must be free to discuss these things within the Christian fellowship (and outside it when it is appropriate to do so). I have occasionally found that some members, especially those from a narrowly Christian background, have welcomed me with evident relief when I have confessed that I have had difficulties with my beliefs. It was as if they had never before had permission to express their doubts openly.

Taking our cue from the Psalmist, we can address our questioning 'Whys' to God. By making them the subject of our approach to the Lord, we maintain our openness to him and demonstrate that we don't want our doubts to spoil his relationship with us; we want him to deal with them according to his gracious purposes.

For faith is not just an intellectual assent to articles of belief such as those listed in the creeds, though intellectual assent is part of it. Nor is it a leap in the dark, though sometimes as believers we have to take risks. No, faith is having confidence in God, and in this confidence trusting our lives to him in union with Jesus Christ.

Doubt, then, is the flipside of faith. It only becomes sinful when we indulge in it. Unless we are careful, we can fall into the temptation of posing as the sort of critic who delights in teasing others about their beliefs, as an unconscious means of coping with our own problems. It is honest to doubt, but faithless to refuse to look beyond our doubts.

If we find that difficult at first, we can look back on our lives and recall what the Holy Spirit has done for us and through us in previous years. Those who keep a diary of their spiritual pilgrimage often find it full of surprises when they re-read what they had written years before. They discover how God guided and equipped them many times in previous years, even though they had not recognized it at the time.

Then we have the witness of other Christians' faith. Living examples of such people are all around us. And the 'cloud of witnesses' from former centuries cheers us, as it were, from heaven. Take a hymn like 'Jesus, the very thought of thee with sweetness fills the breast', written in the twelfth century, possibly by St Bernard of Clairvaux, and then compare it with a contemporary chorus such as, 'Jesus, Name above all names, Blessed Redeemer, Living Lord'. Can such persistent devotion to Jesus' presence and love, experienced across many centuries, cultures and languages, be an illusion?

So prayers about our doubts can lead us to a renewal of faith, as the revelation of God's sovereignty unfolds before us through different sources. Questions can be redeemed if we share them openly with God and tell him what we feel about them. Like Job, we may not be given all the answers, but – again like Job – we shall discover our peace in him restored as his love rekindles our faith.

If we have not had to face doubts ourselves, we shall be in no position to put ourselves alongside other Christians and enquirers who are asking questions about the faith. That is why the Father allowed his Son to enter into the depths of doubt, so that he could be the Redeemer of all those who doubt, too.

Reading

I have been through nearly all my life as a believing Christian, but that does not mean that I have found belief easy. Christian faith has been for me a constant process of wrestling, of losing and finding, of alternating night and day. Faith is a sort of adventurous conflict in the midst of which certainty deepens. When certainty passes, as it does for me, into a sense of peace and serenity, it is nonetheless a costly peace, a peace at the heart of conflict.

Michael Ramsey

Scriptures

You who fear the LORD, praise him!
    All you offspring of Jacob, glorify him;
    stand in awe of him, all you offspring of Israel!
For he did not despise or abhor
    the affliction of the afflicted;
he did not hide his face from me,
    but heard when I cried to him.
From you comes my praise in the great congregation;
    my vows I will pay before those who fear him.

Psalm 22.23–25

My friends, since we have confidence to enter the sanctuary by the blood of Jesus, by the new and living way that he opened for us through the curtain (that is, through his flesh), and since we have a great priest over the house of God, let us approach with a true heart in full assurance of faith, with our hearts sprinkled clean from an evil conscience and our bodies washed with pure water. Let us hold fast to the confession of our hope without wavering, for he who has promised is faithful.

Hebrews 10.19–23

Thomas (who was called the Twin), one of the twelve, was not with them when Jesus came. So the other disciples told him, 'We have seen the Lord.' But he said to them, 'Unless I see the mark of the nails in his hands, and put my finger in the mark of the nails and my hand in his side, I will not believe.' A week later his disciples were again in the house, and Thomas was with them. Although the doors were shut, Jesus came and stood among them and said, 'Peace be with you.'

Then he said to Thomas, 'Put your finger here and see my hands. Reach out your hand and put it in my side. Do not doubt but believe.' Thomas answered him, 'My Lord and my God!'

John 20.24–28

Prayer

You know, Lord, there are nights and days
when doubts suddenly erupt in my mind
and I struggle to hold on to my faith in you.

It is as if there are two spirits inside me,
one wanting to trust you in everything,
the other taunting me with questions.
Like my Saviour on the cross,
I want to ask if you have forsaken me.

When I read of those heroes of the past,
the saints whom you chose
as messengers of the gospel of your Kingdom,
I wonder if they went through tunnels of doubt like mine –
doubts forgotten when their stories were told?

Come, Lord, in the love of your Holy Spirit
and meet me in this darkness;
take me by the hand and lead me back
into the glorious light of your truth.
Forgive me for lingering in those shadows,
and renew me in that first love for you
which I had at the beginning.

Thank you for those women and men
whose lives were built on a faith
which inspired me and manifested to me
the signs of your kingdom.

Guide me on my journey through doubt to faith,
that what I believe with my mind
may become the joy of my heart.
So may I also be your obedient witness
to those making that same journey.

3

Anxiety

Reflections

When C. S. Lewis expressed his worries over a certain matter, a friend reminded him of Jesus' saying about the lilies of the field. 'But lilies don't have feelings!' Lewis replied dryly.

For most of us, life is divided between periods when we feel relatively calm and others when we sense increasing anxiety. It is rather like being on a see-saw, except that more often we find ourselves going down on the anxious side rather than up on the calm one.

Anxiety comes in many different forms. It can be nothing more than a minor uneasiness such as we might have when we have been asked to do something that we haven't done before. At the other extreme it can be a painful anxiety which throws us into a deep depression, causing us to sleep badly, to lose our appetite, and to be in a perpetual state of hopelessness and pessimism. And there are many degrees of anxiety in between.

Provided they are not drastic enough to hinder our normal daily living, certain anxieties are valuable. They can give us a spurt to fulfil a task that we have been avoiding, like cleaning the house before visitors arrive, or paying a bill before we get charged interest. They can also steer us away from taking unnecessary risks, as when we are driving on an over-crowded road or walking along a dangerous footpath.

Other forms of anxiety, such as a teacher might have for

a under-achieving pupil, or a doctor for a patient who is dangerously ill, are laudable signs of professional concern. When a family worries because a member has been suddenly been left a widow, or when parents are apprehensive because their child has been injured on a school skiing holiday, these are the natural reactions of love. Such anxieties have to be accepted as unavoidable in a world where risks sometimes have to be taken. But when anxieties darken our life beyond unavoidable limits, then we need to seek the Lord's help and cry out with the Psalmist, 'Why are you cast down, O my soul, and why are you disquieted within me?' (Psalm 42.5).

We hope that the Lord will help us as we ask questions about our anxiety. Is it caused by a threat to our safety, our personal esteem, our relationship with others? Or by the need to make an important decision about our work, home, or other interests? Or by fear of failure, rejection, intimacy, or conflict? Or is it because we have an excessive concern about our health or our future?

Anxieties can also spring from worries linked in some way with our faith. We may have fears that we are being manipulated by forces outside our control, or God's. We may be anxious because we are coming to believe that the troubles we are experiencing are signs that God is displeased with us. We know intellectually that there are no forces outside God's power, and that he doesn't deliberately inflict us with troubles because of our disobedience (though we bring troubles on ourselves when we do); but it is not always easy to overcome our irrational emotions through rational arguments.

There are various ways of praying through our anxieties. One is to ask God to give us the grace to accept whatever responsibility is involved and to work through it creatively. Another is to invoke the Holy Spirit to strengthen us so that the weakness which causes the anxiety is overcome.

Sometimes, though, I have found it helpful to see my anxiety as a 'target' for my intercessions. I use my imagination to envisage the particular worry (and its deeper cause, if I can discern it) as an object separated from me. I might see it as a dark form which follows me around and refuses to go away. Then, still using my imagination, I grasp the dark form and thrust it away, praying slowly and deliberately along these lines: 'Almighty Father, in Jesus' name I ask you to deliver me from this spirit of . . .' – and here I mention the anxiety – 'that it may trouble me no further. In its place fill me with your peace and restore to me the glorious liberty which in your love you offer to all your children.'

I try to relax physically as I pray this, and imagine the light of the Spirit shining and banishing the dark form and releasing me from the reasons which caused it. This helps me to be more objective about the anxiety and to distance myself from it.

As I have said, the aim of praying in this way is to dissociate myself mentally and emotionally from the cause of the anxiety, and surrendering it to God for him to deal with it. The exercise may sometimes involve praying for healing from earlier experiences which are tied up with the feeling. If there is anything sinful in my life which caused the anxiety, then I need to confess it and seek God's forgiveness through the victory of the cross.

I should add a warning that there is nothing magical about such a prayer. We can offer it only in the faith that the Lord will hear our cry and answer it in his own way and in his own time. We must be prepared to repeat the prayer when the same anxiety keeps coming back to us.

But there are other anxieties which we can resolve by taking practical, commonsense steps to remove them. There is no point in offering anguishing prayers to God if all we need to do is to make a suitable apology, or an appropriate refusal. In any case, many of the worries we have turn out in the end to have been unnecessary. What we had thought would be a difficult encounter with other people becomes, when we meet them, nothing more than a matter of sorting out a misunderstanding.

If, however, an anxiety persists long enough to cast us into a state of recurring or constant depression, it is wise to seek medical advice. There are varieties of clinical depressive syndromes which can be alleviated by a controlled use of drugs prescribed by a doctor. To resort to medical care in such cases is not a sign of a lack of faith; nor should it be a reason for giving up on praying.

A Christian doctor once told me that when a patient came to her surgery to complain of being in a state of constant anxiety, one of the questions the doctor asked, usually after she had prescribed the treatment, was whether the patient had any church connections. If the answer was affirmative, she might gently suggest that the patient invited the priest, the minister or one or two members to pray for him or her. She added that the results of this advice were often very beneficial.

But we can usually be helped when we describe our anxiety to a Christian friend with a listening ear. Their prayers reinforce our own, or they intercede with God when we find it difficult to pray for ourselves. Then we are encouraged to put our anxieties behind us – and become more like the lilies of the field.

Reading

It needs a conscious effort to stop borrowing trouble. Faith and anticipated fear are mutually exclusive. To review the unexpected hurdles of each current day and deliberately give them over to God is a matter of the will. Nothing is gained by worrying all Monday about the meeting one ought to attend on Tuesday. Problems and fears cannot be avoided and should not be denied, but they must not be allowed to take the central place. That belongs to God alone.

Ruth Fowke

Scriptures

The LORD is just in all his ways,
    and kind in all his doings.
The Lord is near to all who call on him,
    to all who call on him in truth.
He fulfils the desire of all who fear him;
    he also hears their cry, and saves them.

Psalm 145.17–19

I am convinced that neither death, nor life, nor angels, nor rulers, nor things present, nor things to come, nor powers, nor height, nor depth, nor anything else in all creation, will be able to separate us from the love of God in Christ Jesus our Lord.

Romans 8.38–39

Jesus said, 'Come to me, all you that are weary and are carrying heavy burdens, and I will give you rest. Take my yoke upon you, and learn from me; for I am gentle and humble in heart, and you will find rest for your souls. For my yoke is easy, and my burden is light.'

Matthew 11.28–30

Prayer

Hold me up, Heavenly Father, as I stumble
in the midst of my anxieties.
Hear my cry and save me.
I shrink from awkward situations
and forceful personalities.

I am haunted by difficulties and tensions;
they are like shadows surrounding me.
I lie awake at night imagining what might happen,
and wondering how I can escape.

Help me to discern between
anxieties which trouble me unnecessarily,
and those which I have to face
because you are calling me
to accept new responsibilities and opportunities.

Your Word assures me
that nothing can separate me from you,
for I am united by your Spirit to Jesus Christ,
who invites me to share my burden with him,
and instead to take his yoke upon my shoulders.

Heal me of the deeper insecurities
which prompt my anxiety.
Banish from me imaginary worries,
and conquer in me those
which are hindering me
from fulfilling the purposes of your kingdom.

4

Anger

Reflections

Most of us are ashamed of getting angry. Afterwards we feel guilty, and we wonder if our friends will despise us for giving way to such a turbulent emotion. Since Jesus commanded us to love one another, we tell ourselves, we should never lose our temper with anyone. We should be forgiving and kindly at all times.

That is a very laudable intention, but it's an unrealistic one. Feelings of anger, even if we try not to show them, are just as natural as being thrilled with good news, or laughing at a humorous situation. Never to be angry would be less than human.

Like all our feelings, anger affects people in different ways. Genetic and hormonal factors play their part; so do the buried memories of abuse or rejection in early childhood. They embody themselves in our subconscious and remain there to affect our attitudes and behaviour until we can find healing for them. In extreme cases they can cause a self-hatred which the sufferers tend to project onto others in moments of stress. After pride, it is the most destructive of all our emotions.

In some of us, anger is sparked instantaneously. A remark, a criticism, a sudden physical pain accidentally inflicted, and our breathing gets faster, our face reddens and our muscles tighten. We feel all churned up inside, and we lash back at those we imagine have offended us. It is a classic example of the fight–flight syndrome.

Others among us are able to suppress our anger temporarily. We 'bottle it up' (a significant analogy). For a while it simmers inside us. Then, when some trivial matter niggles us, the bottle bursts and our anger gushes out on the unfortunate person involved – probably at home among those we love. Suppression can also have other effects: it can bring on a depression, or cause a headache.

We are not entirely to blame if we are tempted to fits of anger, but we are to blame if we don't do anything about them. We need to seek God's help in channelling these strong upsurges of emotion into redemptive thoughts, prayers and worthy activities.

In the Old Testament, God's anger is referred to as his 'wrath'. Behind this phrase was the early attempt of prophets and scribes to teach the people of Israel the gravity of sin and its effects in human terms on their relationship with the Lord. They interpreted it as his righteous anger, and an expression of his love grieving over their disobedience: 'God's love as experienced by the sinner', as it is traditionally called.

This leads to the recognition that there are circumstances when it is permissible for us to be angry. We would be hard-hearted indeed if we did not feel angry about certain things – cruelty to children, or injustice towards individuals and groups. All sorts of godly reforms have sprung from the anger individuals and groups have felt when confronting unjust and cruel situations.

To take one well-known example, it was William Booth's anger at the appalling conditions under which families lived in the East End of London in the last decades of the nineteenth century that stirred him to form the Salvation Army and launch a means of aiding the poor and exploited which still benefits thousands down to our own times.

Such action occurs when anger becomes the inspiration for prayer. As soon as we can in the midst of our raging thoughts, we offer them to God and seek his wisdom in how we are to use them. We might well begin by telling him what we think of the persons or situation which causes us to be angry. But then, as we remember we are approaching the Father through our union with Jesus Christ, who 'himself bore our sins in his body on the cross, so that, free from sins, we might live for righteousness' (1 Peter 2.24), we find the emotion subsiding.

It is at this point that we begin to discern whether our anger was righteous or sinful. The boundary between the two may be blurred at first, because it is often not until afterwards that we can be sure. Generally speaking, if we are angry because we think our pride is being slighted, then that is definitely sinful. Our ego doesn't like being challenged when our opinions are dismissed or our desires are thwarted. When other people have been the recipients of our sinful anger, then we have to seek their forgiveness and confess our sin to God.

But if we discern that in some way our anger reflects what we believe to be God's rejection of wickedness, then it is probably righteous anger which we are experiencing. I add the word 'probably' because many wicked things can be done by those who believe they are fulfilling the divine will, as events in recent years have reminded us. Our surest guide is to place our anger at the foot of the cross. That is where everything, including our emotions, is brought before the judgement of God on all sin.

One of the most testing backlashes of anger is the difficulty of forgiving ourselves. We believe in the forgiveness of God. We experience the forgiveness of others in the joyful reconciliation. But if we have been unjustly angry over some incident in the past, the memory of it springs up long afterwards at unexpected moments, and we are angry with ourselves once more for what we have said and done.

When memories like this recur, we ask God to renew the spiritual gift of repentance, with grace to be humble and more forgiving of ourselves as well as of others. Gradually the memory will cease to trouble us and, as we are reconciled with ourselves, we value even more our reconciliation with God.

Reading

Often what Christ has done and suffered for us has been thought of as something external to us, which we are immensely grateful for but are not intimately involved in. But in truth Christ's sacrifice on the cross is not a substitute for our sacrifice but its seed. The cross has been called and has been represented in art as the tree of life. The fruit of that tree becomes the seed of Christlikeness in us. It is the seed of a growing commitment to God in trust, of a deepening assurance of God's acceptance, of entering more and more into the weakness and vulnerability of Christ crucified, of a growing openness to our fellows.

Christopher Bryant

Scriptures

O LORD my God, I cried to you for help,
    and you have healed me.
Sing praises to the LORD, O you his faithful ones,
    and give thanks to his holy name.
    For his anger is but for a moment;
        his favour is for a lifetime.

Weeping may linger for the night,
  but joy comes with the morning.

Psalm 30.2, 4, 5

Do not grieve the Holy Spirit of God, with which you were marked with a seal for the day of redemption. Put away from you all bitterness and wrath and anger and wrangling and slander, together with all malice, and be kind to one another, tender-hearted, forgiving one another, as God in Christ has forgiven you. Therefore be imitators of God, as beloved children, and live in love, as Christ loved us and gave himself up for us, a fragrant offering and sacrifice to God.

Ephesians 4.30–5.2

Jesus entered the synagogue, and a man was there who had a withered hand. The Pharisees watched him to see whether he would cure him on the sabbath, so that they might accuse him. And he said to the man who had the withered hand, 'Come forward.' Then he said to them, 'Is it lawful to do good or to do harm on the sabbath, to save life or to kill?' But they were silent. He looked around at them with anger; he was grieved at their hardness of heart and said to the man, 'Stretch out your hand.' He stretched it out, and his hand was restored.

Mark 3.1–5

Prayer

Have mercy on me, Father God, when I lose my temper,
and anger towards others surges up within me.
So often pride and fear take possession of me
when I feel I'm being rejected or opposed.

Have mercy on me, too, when I am angry with myself,
When I fail to obey your law of love,
and when, through slothfulness or cowardice,
I turn aside from someone who needs my help.

I know that my anger separates me from you,
and that I deserve your wrath
for grieving your Holy Spirit,
who marked me with your seal of redemption.

I know, too, that it separates me from those I love,
my family, my friends, my church, and those I meet.
I hurt them, as I hurt myself,
and the memory crushes me to the ground.

In spirit I kneel at the foot of the cross,
and confess my sin.
In the name of your beloved Son,
put to death by others' anger,
fill me afresh with gifts of contrition and repentance.

Teach me how I may, in your power,
overcome my weakness.
Give me grace to surrender my anger to you,
that you may transfigure it
into zeal for your righteousness.

5

Sorrow

Reflections

Sorrow is overwhelming when someone dear to us dies – a spouse, a parent, a family member, an old friend. Indeed, we feel as if our lives have shrunk. When my parents died, I was conscious that two very dear links in the chain of my loving relationships had been severed. Grief is particularly sharp and deep when parents or guardians experience the death of their child. It can be a time when the Lord seems very distant.

To understand the painful steps we have to take on our Christian pilgrimage in the midst of personal sorrow, it is helpful to remember that bereavement itself is also a process. Somehow we need to relate our grief process to our spiritual pilgrimage if we are to keep close to God during these empty days. It may not be until some time after the bereavement that we can begin to do this; until then, we may have to rely on the intercessions our friends offer to God for us.

Generally speaking (and one can only speak generally about an individual's thoughts and feelings in the midst of grief) bereavement goes through four stages.

The first is our sense of unreality. 'I can't believe it's hap-pened', we tell ourselves, over and over again. This sense of unreality may last for quite a long time. For weeks after the death of my widowed mother I had to check myself from picking up the phone and dialling her number as I had done regularly when she was alive. Those who have lost children tell me that at first they still listened for the small voice calling them upstairs to tuck them up in bed for the night.

The second stage follows when the realization of what has happened pierces our heart like the thrust of a sword. The loved one really is dead; we shall not see them again in this world. We feel desolated. We have come to the lowest point of the bereavement process.

This stage may last a long time, or it may return again and again years afterwards. Little incidents may trigger these: finding their diary in a drawer, or going back to a favourite holiday place without them. We do not go through the different stages of our bereavement in chronological order; in our grief we can oscillate backwards and forwards from one stage to another.

After a while we slowly emerge into the third stage: acceptance of the fact that, in spite of all that happened, life goes on and we must go with it. We are learning to release the one who has died to God's mercy and love. In our thinking and our expectations we gradually adjust to the fact that they are no longer with us. For some, this stage is reached once the first anniversary of the death has passed.

Eventually we move into the fourth stage: we begin to consider the rest of our lives. Things will never be the same again, but life is still worth living, even though it will be different. New opportunities present themselves. Family, friends, neighbours are still around. We find, though, that our relationship with our family, friends and neighbours may begin to feel different. Especially if we are a widow or a widower, that relationship has changed because we have been used to sharing their company with our spouse. On their side the others may sense the change, too. Showing and expressing sympathy with the bereaved is a sensitive matter. They may not be quite sure how to handle the situation. We can help them by accepting what they have to say with gratitude, and by sharing our feelings with them as freely as we can. That will help to re-establish our relationship.

Practising the presence of God through these stages of bereavement is never easy. As I have said, we may find it difficult to pray at all. There is no need to feel guilty about this. God understands that grieving is perfectly natural; we should not try to suppress grief under the mistaken suspicion that by grieving we are in some way denying our hope in the Lord who has conquered sin and death.

However, during these stages we should try to maintain our normal devotions, even if reading the Bible and the texts of prayers seems an empty exercise. For quite a time the words on the pages mean no more to us than if they were written in an unknown language. But the routine will provide a mental lifeline to the Word of God, even if we don't hear it.

It was an ancient church custom to remember the names of those who had died during the daily masses or other services on the third, seventh and thirtieth days after the funeral, and then on the anniversary each year. In this way the congregation could show their prayer support for the bereaved during the early stages of bereavement. Memorial services after the death fulfil a similar role.

Then one day the scriptures and the texts will shine for us with comforting relevance. It will be as if they are suddenly illuminated from within. A saying from a prophet, a phrase from the New Testament, or the text of a prayer will stir us inwardly with renewed faith and hope. We sense that the Holy Spirit is unfolding the Word of God, encouraging us and pointing us to the promises of Jesus and the love of the Father.

This spiritual breakthrough may help us to move through the third to the fourth stages of the bereavement process. When the next Easter Day arrives, we experience a strange mixture of sadness and joy. Jesus died, too, just as our loved one did. But Jesus rose again, triumphant over sin, suffering and death, the inspiration of our faith and hope.

We may not be sure of our loved one's relationship with God. In any case, it is not our business to judge. What we can do is thank the Lord for the love and goodness they brought into our lives, for such gifts could only have come from heaven. A prayer in memory of the dead commends to God 'those who have died in the faith of Christ, and those whose faith is known to you alone'. We join their names with those of others we have known who have died and for whom we praise God – as I do for my parents and others I have loved.

There can, of course, be lesser bereavements. Sorrow can overtake us at the loss of a job, the departure of a son or daughter from the parental home, even the death of a pet animal. The grieving process will usually be less painful and shorter, perhaps only for a day or two, but the way we pray through the stages of the emotions as we experience them at the time is basically the same.

Reading

Our prayer is greatly influenced by what our bodies and spirits are experiencing. When we do not have a desire to pray, it does not mean that we have lost our faith or that we are being unfaithful to God or that God has forsaken us. Rather, it means that we are experiencing loss, and are at the bend in the road, feeling drained, hollow, empty, spent. That is why our faith and prayer every single day is so important. It enables us to develop a strong union with God . . . Then, when times of loss are weighing heavily on our hearts and we do not have a sense of God's presence, we can fall back on the steadfast belief that God always keeps his vigil over us.

Joyce Rupp

Scriptures

How long, O LORD? Will you forget me for ever?
How long will you hide your face from me?
How long must I bear pain in my soul,
  and have sorrow in my heart all day long? . . .
But I trusted in your steadfast love;
  my heart shall rejoice in your salvation.
I will sing to the LORD,
  because he has dealt bountifully with me.

Psalm 13.1–2, 5–6

Blessed be the God and Father of our Lord Jesus Christ! By his great mercy he has given us a new birth into a living hope through the resurrection of Jesus Christ from the dead, and into an inheritance that is imperishable, undefiled, and unfading, kept in heaven for you, who are being protected by the power of God through faith for a salvation ready to be revealed in the last time.

1 Peter 1.3–5

When Mary came where Jesus was and saw him, she knelt at his feet and said to him, 'Lord, if you had been here, my brother Lazarus would not have died.' When Jesus saw her weeping, and the Jews who came with her also weeping, he was greatly disturbed in spirit and deeply moved. He said, 'Where have you laid him?' They said to him, 'Lord, come and see.' Jesus began to weep. So the Jews said, 'See how he loved him!' But some of them said, 'Could not he who opened the eyes of the blind man have kept this man from dying?'

John 11.32–37

Prayer

Heavenly Father,
loving and strong to save,
be with me as I walk in the shades of sorrow.
You know that N's love and companionship
meant so much to me over all these years.
I cannot imagine what my life will be like in the future.
I feel as if a part of my heart has died with him/her.

When I try to pray, my mind is filled with a picture of N,
memories of the times we had together
and joy of one another's company.
I have no sense of your presence.
Do I have to bear sorrow in my heart all day long?
Yet I know from your Word that you are always with me,
for we have been given a new birth into a living hope
by the resurrection of your Son from the dead.

May your Holy Spirit come over me,
and change my sorrow into hope as I remember N.
Lead me into the sanctuary of your presence
where I can offer in Jesus
my heart in thanksgiving to you, Father,
for the love and goodness you revealed to me
through those who have died in your faith,
and those whose faith is known to you alone.

6

Loneliness

Reflections

Some people, especially those with busy and satisfying occupations, choose to live alone. They appreciate the freedom of being able to make decisions without having to consider anyone else.

But many have not chosen to live that way. They are left by themselves through the death of a husband or wife, a family member or a friend who has shared their home. Suddenly the house is empty; there is no one to talk to. As an elderly lady from Yorkshire, who once lived next door to us with her sister, said sorrowfully to us after the sister had died, 'It wore nice t'ave someone make you a cuppa tea when you cum 'ome.'

Even those who have chosen to live alone may have pangs of envy when they see their relatives and friends with their families; and when they retire from their busy and satisfying occupations, and age and infirmity restrict their activities, a chilly sense of loneliness begins to creep in.

It can be a moment of choice for us. If we turn up one road, we can become preoccupied with ourselves and our own welfare. We try to compensate for our loneliness by trivial and maybe expensive distractions, and become addicted to TV-watching, alcohol or drugs. Our selfishness increases and we begin to see friends and neighbours not only as welcome visitors, but also people we try to manipulate for our own purposes. An ancient wisdom writer issued a warning about this: 'The one who lives alone is self-indulgent, showing contempt for all who have sound judgement' (Proverbs 18.1).

But if we turn up the other road, we can accept our loneliness as a new opportunity to respond to God's call in our lives. Looking away from ourselves and trusting in his guidance, we may discover that he opens up our personal horizons in unexpected and interesting ways. We wake up each morning with the expectation that that particular day will be unique in all that the Lord has for us.

Living alone presents us with opportunities for resting in the presence of God, which are not so easy to enjoy when we are distracted by others in the house. We have a relationship with him which can only be weakened on our side by selfishness and disobedience; it is not broken by feelings of loneliness. God is always with us, whether our loneliness is chosen or forced upon us.

Many Christians think of the divine presence in terms of 'Jesus-and-me'. The words of some popular hymns and choruses reinforce this concept. Devotion to the person of Jesus as our Saviour and Lord is, of course, where most of us begin our pilgrimage; the stories of his saving work in the Gospels are an approach to appreciating his presence with us. I certainly don't want to write anything which seems to undermine that loving vision. But it is spiritually enriching to remember that we are not only in a one-to-one relationship with Jesus; we are also in a relationship of 'Three-to-one-with-many'.

What I mean is this. The *Three* are the Persons of the Holy Trinity. The scriptures teach us that our union with Jesus through baptism also draws us into the communion he has with the Father and the Holy Spirit. It was in the name of the Trinity that we were baptized. The mystery of God's Being is revealed through the scriptures as they were meditated on, and their truth experienced, by the Church's early teachers. The mystery remains beyond human comprehension, but the revelation was sufficient for us to understand that when we approach the Father through Christ we are being drawn by the Holy Spirit into a community of divine Persons.

The famous Andrei Rublev icon was painted about the year 1410 as a representation of the visit of the three angels to Abraham at the oak of Mamre, but it is interpreted as a pictorial meditation on the Trinity. It shows three figures sitting at a table. Jesus, facing the viewer, is at the back looking at the Father on his right; on his left is the Holy Spirit gazing at the other two. The icon suggests various things for us to meditate on, but what is most striking for our purpose is that the front of the table is left unoccupied, as if inviting us to approach and join the divine circle.

The *one* is me – ourselves. It is the Spirit who urges us forwards and Christ who welcomes us to the icon's table to present us to the Father. It is a profoundly humbling and awe-inspiring thought. We feel both unworthy and privileged, and we want to repent and to praise. It is the place where prayer begins.

But we do not do this alone, even if we are by ourselves. The *many* are those to whom the Spirit unites us in Christ: the fellowship of all those who have been, are, and will be faithful to the Lord. We are one of countless members of the Body of Christ: 'Fellow-heirs, members of the same body, and sharers in the promise in Christ Jesus through the gospel' (Ephesians 3.6). The traditional introduction to the *Sanctus* spreads out the vast panorama of this fellowship beyond this life: 'Therefore with angels and archangels, and with all the company of heaven, we proclaim your great and glorious name . . .'

Our faith is strengthened as we reflect on scriptural passages which are the first unfolding of the pages of this mystery, and as we read printed prayers, especially those which are Trinitarian in pattern. We recollect the fellowship we have in Christ with his Church, especially those we know and love. Paul echoed this faith in his benediction: 'The grace of our Lord Jesus Christ, the love of God, and the communion of the Holy Spirit be with all of you' (2 Corinthians 13.13). It is difficult to go on feeling lonely with such an assurance coming to us across the ages.

Such prayers can also be helpful for those who are inwardly lonely – that is, individuals who live with a family or friends but who, through circumstances beyond their control, find themselves shut out from closer intimacy. This can be the assurance of those who are the only Christian in a non-christian household, or one of another religion. They are unable to share with the others the faith they have in God; consequently at home their devotions are lonely experiences, to be kept private and not discussed and enjoyed with those they live with. Their greatest hope is that, through their prayers and their relationships, the Holy Spirit will enlighten the minds of the others and bring them to believe in Jesus Christ as their Lord and Saviour, too.

Reading

The Father is present with us as the Source of all life. The Word is the communicative, who speaks as the only Word of the Father, and through the Holy Spirit we can not only hear God's Word of love and power, but we will also be empowered by ever-deepening faith, hope and love of the Spirit to respond to the Word. The Holy Spirit is the mutual love proceeding from the Father to the Son, and vice versa. The Spirit unites himself to my free will to bring me into the supernatural love of the Father and the Son.

George A. Maloney

Scriptures

O God, you are my God, I seek you,
   my soul thirsts for you;
my flesh faints for you,
  as in a dry and weary land where there is no water.
So I have looked upon you in the sanctuary,
   beholding your power and glory.
Because your steadfast love is better than life,
   my lips will praise you.
So I will bless you as long as I live;
   I will lift up my hands and call on your name.
My soul is satisfied as with a rich feast.

Psalm 63.1–5

Blessed be the God and Father of our Lord Jesus Christ, the Father of mercies and the God of all consolation, who consoles us in all our affliction, so that we may be able to console those who are in any affliction with the consolation with which we ourselves are consoled by God.

2 Corinthians 1.3–4

Jesus ordered the crowds to sit down on the grass. Taking the five loaves and the two fish, he looked up to heaven, and blessed and broke the loaves, and gave them to the disciples, and the disciples gave them to the crowds. And all ate and were filled; and they took up what was left over of the broken pieces, twelve baskets full. And those who ate were about five thousand men, besides women and children. Immediately he made the disciples get into the boat and go on ahead to the other side, while he dismissed the crowds.

And after he had dismissed the crowds, he went up the mountain by himself to pray.

Matthew 14.19–23

Prayer

Heavenly Father,
as I look round the four walls of my room,
I see familiar things which remind me
of families and friends, past and present,
and of all that these dear folk have meant to me.
I praise you for the love and companionship
I have received, and still receive, from them.

Yet this feeling of loneliness,
creeps round me like a chill.
I feel as if I am in a dry and weary land
where there is no water.

Anoint me afresh with your Holy Spirit:
rescue me from self-pity;
fire my imagination with thoughts and pictures
which take me in spirit beyond these walls
to the fellowship of your people,
here in this neighbourhood and beyond.

I want to join the crowds on the grass
as Jesus speaks to us and satisfies our hunger,
remembering the many times
I've shared the Bread and Wine
at your table in church with your people.

Feed me with the joy of your presence,
and strengthen in me the truth
that nothing can separate you from me,
not even feelings of isolation,
Father, Son and Holy Spirit.

7

Guilt

Reflections

My first memory of personal guilt is a lie I told in my first year at primary school. I said it to avoid being blamed for misbehaviour I had caused on the bus going home. I can still picture the look of reproach on my teacher's face when she learned the truth. From that moment I knew what it was to feel guilty.

I think it was from about then that I also came to recognize my conscience as a kind of warning bell when I strayed, or was tempted to stray, from the path of righteousness. T. S. Eliot described our conscience as the power to feel our thoughts and think our feelings on moral issues. It is our mind making moral judgements. Looked at from a biblical perspective, our conscience is the organ through which we may hear the voice of the Holy Spirit, acting as our guide in the choices which confront us every day.

Like other faculties, our conscience requires educating. Being brought up in a Christian home is a good beginning. After our home, the best environment for this continuing education is the fellowship of the Church. There we can draw on the resources which the Spirit makes available to us through the Bible, sound teaching, discussion, prayer, worship, sacraments and the fellowship of other Christians. Beyond the Church we sometimes find our consciences enlightened further through contact with other good and wise people of other faiths or none.

Conscience warns us when we are being tempted and what kind of a sin is tempting us. There are sins of commission and sins of omission. Then there are sins committed, in the words of a general confession used in church services, 'through negligence, through weakness, and through our own deliberate fault'.

These three categories represent: things we say or do but only learn afterwards that they are sinful (through negligence, because we have not taken the trouble to find out); sins which are the result of a momentary lapse on our part (through personal weakness); and those which we choose to commit even though we know we are doing wrong (through our own deliberate fault).

Christian moralists tell us that these categories are only rough-and-ready distinctions, and that what may be a serious lapse for one individual may not, in certain circumstances, be so serious for another. But however that may be, when we sin, feelings of guilt sweep over us as we realize that we have fallen short of what God requires of us.

Although I have called guilt a 'feeling', it is more than that. It is an aching disturbance within us at a spiritual level; it is our inner being as a child of God fearful and grieving over our rejection of his love. When we 'come to ourselves' we know we have turned our backs on the cross, which won for us the forgiveness of sins and a new life in Jesus Christ; we know that it is our pride which has tempted us to 'do it our way' rather than God's way.

That feeling – and more than a feeling – of guilt can provide the energy for turning back to the Lord. We don't need to linger in it. We can use it as a means of seeking the Spirit's gift of repentance. Compare it to surfing on a West Country beach. The guilt is like the breakers rolling in from the sea. As one of them rushes up to us, we mount the board and launch ourselves into it so that it carries us forwards. The wave of guilt now becomes the gift of repentance which we are seeking. Eventually we find ourselves cast on the sands at the foot of the cross where we ask for God's forgiveness.

It must have been some such wave of guilt that led to the Psalmist's well-known cry for forgiveness: 'Have mercy on me, O God, according to your steadfast love; according to your abundant mercy blot out my transgressions' (Psalm 51.1). Once we acknowledge our guilt and confess our sin, God responds by restoring us, like the father in the parable who runs out to greet his home-coming prodigal son.

However, though the grace of God's forgiveness is free, it is not cheap. It cost his Son the agony and death of Calvary. For us it involves the cost of reparation. We are not completely forgiven in heaven unless we have done all we reasonably can to be forgiven on earth. If our sin has caused great pain to our neighbour, or has wounded our family, or has damaged the reputation of our church, then we must ask for their forgiveness, too (and, of course, be willing to forgive them if and when the circumstances are reversed, as the petition in the Lord's Prayer constantly directs us).

Even then, it is unrealistic to expect them to welcome us back as if nothing had happened. Part of our reparation may be having to accept the fact that our relationship with them has been damaged and that it may be some time before, under God's guidance, full reconciliation takes place. If and when we begin to feel exasperated by the delay, that calls for patience on our side and understanding on theirs.

We also need to invoke the Spirit to strengthen us against temptations which lead us into sin in the future. We may fail often, but a sincere confession is never rejected by God, and with perseverance we shall in time enjoy the victory.

There are rare occasions when we suddenly remember a particular sin we committed maybe years ago. We confessed at the time, we believed we were forgiven, we were reconciled with those we offended, but the memory of it flashes back into our minds long after we had forgotten it. This experience usually means that we have not entirely forgiven ourselves. Then it becomes an opportunity to thank God again for the mercy he showed us at the time, and to ask him to give us his peace.

But if it persists, as it may do if we are over-scrupulous, we may be wise to talk about it with a trusted Christian friend, or go to a priest or an ordained minister and seek their advice. A prayer for deliverance from the effects of the memory, or an absolution pronounced by the priest or minister may be the appropriate means of burying the memory.

Finally, there are often certain grey areas between discerning what is offensive to God and what is pleasing to him. The speed of change in scientific medicine, to take one example, makes this particularly difficult. Even Christian moralists disagree among themselves on certain things. In the end we have to try and decide for ourselves between what is acceptable to God in our culture and what is not, and be guided by our conscience to act accordingly.

Reading

The laying down of human life that took place on Calvary was more than enough to outweigh all human sins, because that life belonged to the second person of the Trinity. This was God's marvellous plan: human sins should be atoned for by one of the human family who would be capable of obtaining such forgiveness because he was also God . . . But that is not all. Because Jesus is our representative, when he died, all whom he represented also died. We did not die ourselves, we died *in him*. This is the important truth – *we died in him*.

Ian Pettit

Scriptures

Bless the LORD, O my soul,
   and all that is within me,
   bless his holy name.
Bless the LORD, O my soul,
   and do not forget all his benefits –
who forgives all your iniquity,
   who heals all your diseases.
For as the heavens are high above the earth,
   so great is his steadfast love towards those who fear him;
as far as the east is from the west,
   so far he removes our transgressions from us.
As a father has compassion for his children,
   so the LORD has compassion for those who fear him.

Psalm 103.1–3, 11–13

The word of God is living and active, sharper than any two-edged sword, piercing until it divides soul from spirit, joints from marrow; it is able to judge the thoughts and intentions of the heart. And before him no creature is hidden, but all are naked and laid bare to the eyes of the one to whom we must render an account. Since, then, we have a great high priest who has passed through the heavens, Jesus, the Son of God, let us hold fast to our confession. For we do not have a high priest who is unable to sympathize with our weaknesses, but we have one who in every respect has been tested as we are, yet without sin. Let us therefore approach the throne of grace with boldness, so that we may receive mercy and find grace to help in time of need.

Hebrews 4.12–16

When the scribes and Pharisees kept on questioning Jesus [about the woman taken in adultery], he straightened up and said to them, 'Let anyone among you who is without sin be the first to throw a stone at her.' And once again he bent down and wrote on the ground. When they heard it, they went away, one by one, beginning with the elders; and Jesus was left alone with the woman standing before him. Jesus straightened up and said to her, 'Woman, where are they? Has no one condemned you?' She said, 'No one, sir.' And Jesus said, 'Neither do I condemn you. Go your way, and from now on do not sin again.'

John 8.7–11

Prayer

Loving Father, I know that you love me
with a tenderness and desire
far beyond anything I can imagine or feel.
I recognize that every time I allow
temptations to overwhelm me,
I grieve you by rejecting your love
and spoil our relationship.

My conduct falls far short of what I promised
when I became your child by baptism.
I recognize, too, that in my sin

I have separated myself
from those joined to me in the Body of your Son
and caused pain among them, too.

Trusting in the power of your Holy Spirit,
I beg for your forgiveness
and ask in Jesus' name for the gift of repentance.
I desire to renounce all temptations to sinfulness,
and through your loving mercy
be reconciled once again to you.

I ask, too, for your wisdom and patience
in seeking the pardon of
those I have offended.
May they be willing to receive me once again
so that our union in Christ may be restored.

Help me to learn a new humility
and to serve you as a forgiven sinner
who rejoices in the blessing of your mercy and love.

8

Regret

⮂

Reflections

Feelings of regret extend beyond any feelings of guilt we might have. We feel guilty when we know we have sinned against God and against our neighbour. But we can continue to have regrets long after we have experienced forgiveness and reconciliation – regrets that we allowed ourselves to get into the situation where we were tempted and fell into sin.

When I was in the Army a group of us who were to be drafted overseas were given an orientation course one day to prepare us for what we might expect once we were posted. One of the lectures was given by the garrison chaplain who, among other things, warned us of the dangers of sexual immorality. The only thing I remember of what he said were his words, 'Don't do anything which you will regret for years afterwards.'

There was a murmur of uneasy amusement round the room as the men realized the implications of what he was saying. He was pointing out that there was not only the possibility of our contracting venereal disease; we might also unwittingly father a child, and the knowledge that such a child existed could haunt us for the rest of our lives.

Similar regrets can haunt women who have abortions. I have met a few who had a pregnancy terminated when they were young. Often they were in a desperate situation and believed there was no alternative solution to their problem. If they were Christians – or, more often, if they were converted years afterwards – they confessed that they had done wrong and were assured that they were forgiven, but they still mourned for the loss of the child and regretted the decision. In one or two cases the feelings of regret still lingered in their old age.

This is the aftermath of any kind of sin, especially grievous ones. The memory stays with us, even if it is dimmed with the passage of time. At unlooked-for moments the familiar pang of regret touches our heart once more, and we wish we could re-write that bit of our personal story.

Regrets, however, are not only associated with sins confessed and forgiven. They creep up to us when we look back and realize that, when a particular opportunity offered itself, we might have made a better choice. Perhaps we made the decision in a hurry, or maybe we thought we did not have the ability to take up an offer of a job made to us, so we turned it down. Then, for years afterwards, we look back in sadness at the lost opportunity. These kinds of choices were hardly of an ethical nature; they simply seemed right at the time. But they survive as the 'might-have-beens' and 'if onlys' which ruffle our peace of mind now and then.

More poignant are memories of lost opportunities of showing our affection for those we have loved before they died. Such regrets are closely linked with mourning their deaths. They are a part of the bereavement process.

My eighty-nine-year-old widowed mother, who lived by herself about fifty miles away from us, used to ring us up regularly every Sunday afternoon for a chat. One Sunday the phone was silent. As I had visited her the previous day, I assumed she had decided not to make her usual call. That night the local hospital rang to tell me that a friend had visited my mother in the late afternoon and found her slumped in her chair with the telephone receiver in her hand;

she must have been about to ring us when she lost consciousness. She had been taken to the hospital by ambulance and died a few hours later. I shall always regret that I did not phone her to discover why she had not called us. Had I done so, each time I dialled her number I would have heard the 'engaged' signal and guessed something was wrong.

We cannot banish such regrets, for they are closely interwoven with the bonds of affection we have for those who have died. But faith in the boundless love and power of God can help us to see our regrets, not as dead ends about which we can do nothing, but steps on our pilgrimage to trust more in the Lord.

Towards the end of the Old Testament story of Joseph there is a saying which is a word of wisdom for us in this situation. His brothers sold him as a slave to Egypt, but after a series of adventures he became chief minister under the Pharaoh and saved the land from famine. When the brothers came to Egypt to buy corn they met Joseph again and, at his invitation, migrated to Egypt with their families and their elderly father, Jacob. But when Jacob died, the brothers were afraid Joseph might take his revenge on them, so they told him that before he died the father had instructed them to tell Joseph that he (Jacob) wanted him (Joseph) to forgive his brothers for what they had done to him years previously. Joseph assured them he had forgiven them, and then, pointing out how he had prospered in Egypt, added, 'Even though you intended to do harm to me, God intended it for good' (Genesis 50.20).

What is so inspired about this saying is that it prophetically reveals a truth about the sovereignty of God – that even the awful consequences of sin may, in time, be turned round to fulfil his divine purpose. It is a theme which runs throughout the Old Testament and finds its climax in the greatest sin of all – the crucifixion of the Son of Man – which became the means of salvation for all of us. An anthem sung on Good Friday echoes this: 'We glory in your cross, O Lord, and praise you for your mighty resurrection, for by virtue of your cross joy has come into our world.'

Some regrets will remain unresolved all our days. Perhaps only in the light of eternity will we come to see they had their purpose in our life and in the lives of others. But in spite of this, we trust that God will take the things we regret and 'intend them for good'.

As we get older, we begin to see signs of this in certain cases, though not all. That unloving word, or that selfish act of which we are ashamed, eventually leads in a strange and unexpected manner to something creative or joyful. The wrong choice we made years ago is cancelled out by a wise choice which we made years later – perhaps having learned from our previous mistake. If feelings of regret never entirely die, they can have about them a hint of resurrection which lifts the burden of them from us, so that in time they are mingled with our feelings of thankfulness.

Reading

I have to ask forgiveness for many things. I suppose it is wrong to say that one is glad to need it, and yet I must confess to that very creaturely feeling. And if ever I honestly had the chance of forgiving someone something very real, it would be, I feel sure, a very high kind of happiness. I am sure forgiving is one of God's greatest joys.

Father Andrew

Scriptures

In you, O LORD, I seek refuge;
    do not let me ever be put to shame;
    in your righteousness deliver me.
Incline your ear to me;
    rescue me speedily.
Be a rock of refuge for me,
    a strong fortress to save me.
You are indeed my rock and my fortress;
    for your name's sake lead me and guide me,
take me out of the net that is hidden for me,
    for you are my refuge.
Into your hand I commit my spirit;
    you have redeemed me, O LORD, faithful God.

Psalm 31.1–5

The Spirit helps us in our weakness; for we do not know how to pray as we ought, but that very Spirit intercedes with sighs too deep for words. And God, who searches the heart, knows what is the mind of the Spirit, because the Spirit intercedes for the saints according to the will of God. We know that all things work together for good for those who love God, who are called according to his purpose.

Romans 8.26–28

As Jesus walked along, he saw a man blind from birth. His disciples asked him, 'Rabbi, who sinned, this man or his parents, that he was born blind?' Jesus answered, 'Neither this man nor his parents sinned; he was born blind so that God's works might be revealed in him.'

John 9.1–3

Prayer

Heavenly Father,
you have forgiven, strengthened and guided me
all through the years of my life.
You have been my rock of refuge and a strong fortress
to save me from sin and foolishness.

Yet memories of my disobediences and mistakes
return to me when I least expect them.
I remember temptations
I could have resisted in your strength,
and choices which diverted me from the path
along which your Holy Spirit was leading.
The memories linger and put me to shame.
I regret my weakness and stupidity
which led to what I said and did.

In the name of Jesus,
I ask you to search my heart
and lift the burden from me.
In your righteousness may I receive
wisdom to learn from my past errors.

I dare to ask that, because your Word reveals
you can take the consequences of our sins and mistakes
and, through our repentance and faith,
intend them for good.
Guide my thoughts, words and deeds in the future,
so that my regrets may become
a source of thankfulness instead of shame.

9

Contentment

Reflections

The word 'content' is linked with 'contain'. It describes what is contained in something. The first pages of a book include a list of the contents to help a reader see at a glance the sort of material it contains. If the contents page has been compiled accurately, it will be sufficient to fulfil its purpose when a reader uses it.

To be content, then, is to feel fulfilled, to feel we have what is required for life to be worthwhile. We are in reasonably good health. Our relationships with family and friends are free of any upsets. We feel materially secure, and we are at peace with ourselves. All seems right with our world, and there is nothing in the immediate future we can think of which threatens to disturb us. That is contentment: in contemporary jargon, 'well-being'.

But such a feeling rarely lasts for long. Other emotions, such as some of those listed in this book, threaten to intrude into our peace. We become ill, our relationship with a friend breaks down, or our personal security is jeopardized, and suddenly our contentment vanishes. We realize that the things we relied on for our peace of mind are letting us down.

In every age, teachers of ethics have urged their students not to rely on this world's goods for their contentment. They have pointed out that those who seek wealth and power have rarely found happiness when they have achieved them. Plutarch said, 'Learn to be pleased with everything; with wealth, so far as it makes us beneficial to others; with poverty, with not having too much to care for; and with obscurity, for being unenvied.'

Humanist teachers, however, are less than helpful in showing their followers where they can find the resources for such contentment. They have usually advised their students to exercise self-mastery through ascetic exercises and to be encouraged by the example of others. But Christians, knowing that self-mastery is unachievable for sinful men and women, have learned that only in God is true peace to be found.

Preparing his disciples for the end of his earthly ministry, Jesus said to them: 'Peace I leave with you; my peace I give to you. I do not give to you as the world gives. Do not let your hearts be troubled, and do not let them be afraid' (John 14.27). While Paul was under house arrest in Rome, he received a visitor from the church in Philippi. This congregation was rather special to him; it was the first one he had founded when he crossed into Macedonia and entered Europe, and they had been supportive after he left them to continue his mission. Hearing of the apostle's imprisonment, they were concerned for his welfare and sent Epaphroditus with gifts (presumably money). One of his reasons for writing his letter to the Philippians was to thank them.

So that they would not be unduly anxious, he assured them, 'I have learned to be content with whatever I have. I know what it is to have little, and I know what it is to have plenty. In any and all circumstances I have learned the secret of being well-fed and of going hungry, of having plenty and of being in need.' The reason he was content, he told them, was that he relied totally upon God. 'I can do all things through him who strengthens me.' But then, perhaps realizing they might feel he was being a little dismissive of what they had done for him, he added, 'In any case, it was kind of you to share my distress' (Philippians 4.11–14).

Jealousy is a great enemy of contentment. Our desire in wanting to do better than others is stimulated by the competitive culture with which we are surrounded, and the consumerism which animates everything thrown at us by the media. It takes discernment and courage to resist these temptations and keep our desire fixed on the Lord.

Contentment is not the same as complacency. There are things which we can never be content with if we are true to the gospel. Sin in all its forms, in ourselves as well as in society, is to be resisted. There may be occasions when we must refute untruths or oppose injustices. Outwardly these initiatives may cause trouble and maybe pain in our lives; but if our sole desire is to be obedient to God, then these outward disturbances will not take away the inner peace he gives us. And, above all, we can never be content with our side of our relationship with him.

There resides in some Christians a rather childish hope that, if they are obedient to God's commandments, he will reward them with special favours, including good health and material prosperity. Then, when things go wrong, and they are ill or become poorer, they are disappointed. They had expected him to protect them from the pains and tragedies of life; and when he apparently doesn't, they feel cheated.

Their error is that they have lapsed into complacency. They have forgotten that in responding to Jesus' call we have to be prepared to accept the sacrifices which that involves, as he warned us, 'Whoever does not carry the cross and follow me cannot be my disciple' (Luke 14.27). The victory of God's kingdom is assured – that is the basis for our contentment – but in the journey to the kingdom we are not immune from the realities of daily life. What we learn from the gospel is that, whatever happened to Jesus, he never lost his sense of oneness with his heavenly Father, which was the secret of his inner peace. That peace he offered to his followers, and Paul was one who accepted it through suffering as well as joy.

True, we go through times when unhappy experiences cause us to ask ourselves if we have made mistakes. We may be tempted to wonder if we have failed the Lord in some way. If we have been trying to live our Christian life as sincerely as we can, there is no need to feel ashamed. Instead, we should review our past and present situation and re-examine it. Quite likely, nothing that was obviously unworthy of our calling occurs to us – or, at the most, we may see that certain adjustments have to be made – and we accept the uncertainties as an opportunity to renew our trust in God. It is the common experience of Christ's followers that they are tested from time to time by circumstances, or are the subject of some spiritual attack.

'You will always have to work at your marriage', a wise preacher said to the couple at their wedding service; 'there must never be a day when you take each other for granted.'

That is also sound advice about our relationship with God. For Paul, it was like running a race (1 Corinthians 9.24). For Peter, it was growing up in our salvation (1 Peter 2.2). What gives the greatest sense of contentment is the discovery that, as we commit ourselves more and more to Jesus, he is present with us by his Spirit. Then in the depths of our consciousness there grows contentment unlike anything else we experience. It is a sign of the peace of God which passes all understanding, and that is the greatest treasure of all.

Reading

Our dignity is that we are children of God, capable of communion with God, the object of God's love – displayed to us on the cross – and destined for eternal fellowship with God.

Our true value is not what we are worth in ourselves, but what we are worth to God, and that worth is bestowed upon us by the utterly gratuitous love of God.

William Temple

Scriptures

For the LORD God is a sun and a shield;
 he bestows favour and honour.
No good thing does the Lord withhold
 from those who walk uprightly.
O LORD of hosts,
 happy is everyone who trusts in you.

Psalm 84.11–12

Keep your lives free from the love of money, and be content with what you have; for he has said, 'I will never leave you or forsake you.' So we can say with confidence, 'The Lord is my helper; I will not be afraid. What can anyone do to me?'

Hebrews 13.5–6

Jesus said to his disciples, 'The kingdom of heaven is like treasure hidden in a field, which someone found and hid; then in his joy he goes and sells all that he has and buys that field. Again, the kingdom of heaven is like a merchant in search of fine pearls; on finding one pearl of great value, he went and sold all that he had and bought it.'

Matthew 13.44–46

Prayer

Jesus, it was the Father's will
that you should become poor that I might become rich.
You rejected the honours and powers
this world might have showered upon you,
and received a crown of thorns
that I might be offered the treasures of your kingdom.

Forgive me for those days when I was jealous
of those who seemed to enjoy
more of this world's good than I do.
Deliver me from the complacency
which shuns the sacrifice of discipleship.
Banish from my hopes and thoughts any suggestion
I am worth any reward except
that of knowing that I am doing your will.

May I respond with love to the great love,
which took you to the cross and offered me eternal life.
May the fire of your Holy Spirit
purify my selfish desires, ambitions and jealousies.
Lead me into a life of obedience,
which brings your gift of peace to those
who surrender their hearts to you.

10

Hope

❧

Reflections

The word 'hope' brings two pictures into my mind. One is of a queue which forms every Saturday in our local super-market. They are people waiting to buy their tickets for the National Lottery for the draw that evening.

The other is of a procession which used to place in Liverpool at Pentecost each year. It was made up of hundreds of Christians demonstrating that, in spite of their denomina-tional differences, they were growing together into the unity for which Jesus Christ prayed. The procession went between the Anglican and the Roman Catholic cathedrals in the city, and on the two or three occasions when I joined it, I looked up at the sign giving the name of the street along which we were walking and singing: it was the well-known 'Hope Street'. The two pictures illustrate for me the distinction between uncertain hope and certain hope. The first looks to what this world offers; the second trusts in the promises of God.

Although hope in what the world offers is uncertain, there's nothing wrong in hoping for what is good and worth-while in it. We hope we shall not have to cancel a holiday because of unexpected circumstances. We hope that our friends who are getting married will be happy, or that our children will do well at school. We hope for a long and healthy life.

Such hopes are quite normal. But we need to be realistic about them. Unexpected circumstances can ruin our holiday. Marriages can go through difficult phases. Not all children do well at school. Lives are not always long and healthy. If we don't accept those limitations, disappointment can mar our lives. 'Hope deferred makes the heart sick' (Proverbs 13.12).

Jesus' teaching about hope has nothing to do with worldly prospects. It is as far removed as possible from any idea of an earthly utopia or wishful thinking. Rather, in his teaching and in the apostolic writings, hope is an aspect of faith which gives us confidence that God cares for us and for the world he has created. This intimate relationship between hope and faith is nowhere more clearly expressed than in the letter to the Hebrews: 'Now faith is the assurance of things hoped for, the conviction of things not seen' (11.1).

But this can be a struggle when we face misfortunes and painful experiences in our lives and in the lives of others. The person who says, 'Let's hope for the best' may have a cheerful disposition, but he or she may also be a victim of superficiality. The reality is that misfortunes and painful experiences can undermine our hope unless that hope is grounded in our faith in Jesus Christ.

In recent years we have been able to read or listen to accounts given by men and women who have been captured as hostages as a result of the hostilities in the Middle East. In almost every case they said that what made the imprisonment bearable was hope of rescue. It was that hope which gave them the vitality to endure their circumstances. Those who were Christians tried to look beyond the possibility of rescue and set their hope on God and his love for them.

Some former hostages report that when their fellow prisoners lost hope, they deteriorated mentally and ceased to care for themselves or for others. They sank into a state of deep depression which gradually buried their desire to live. For life and hope are intimately linked. Without hope there is little reason for living. The phrase 'Live in hope' can be turned round: 'In hope is life'. It is noteworthy that 'aspiration', a synonym of 'hope', takes its meaning from the concept of 'drawing breath'.

We can be full of hope while at the same time developing a clear and level-headed view of our own inadequacies and those of the world around us. We believe that God can do great things through us, and that gives us hope, but it does not mean we can dream the impossible dream. Among the many inadequacies of the world, we should be particularly aware of the effect of much of the news fed to us by the media. Good news does not sell newspapers, nor does it make dramatic TV pictures. The unrelieved diet of crises, tragedies and conflict leave many, especially the most vulnerable among us, nervous and depressed.

Furthermore, our natural disposition also affects our feelings of hope. People react differently to the way life treats them. Some will have a deep and joyful thankfulness for what they experience. Others will have to struggle against their innate pessimism. And others will summon up their ability not to become embittered and full of rancour.

Whatever our disposition, however, we need to be aware of its effect on us, and pray for it to be cleansed and healed by the power of the Holy Spirit. For hope is a gift of the Spirit, and when he comes to us with that gift, it transfigures the natural aspirations to happiness which God has placed in our hearts; it takes them up and redirects them towards the kingdom of heaven.

In this way, our feelings of hope become expressions of our faith. They give us an outlook on life which is quite different from the natural disposition of optimism. Our hope becomes grounded in thankfulness for God's purposes for his world, and for his Church and its ministry in the world. So hope and faith lead to a life in which we try to reflect the love of God in all we say and do – Paul's famous triad of faith, hope and love.

And hope gives us faith for God's loving purposes for us beyond this life, too. Looking beyond death, faith in the resurrection of Christ builds up our hope for eternal life with him. We may shrink from the thought of physically dying, but we trust in scriptural revelation that, through our baptismal union with Jesus, we are already enjoying the first-fruits of eternity here and now. Then, through his mercy and grace, we shall be ready for the fulfilment of our hope when in the Spirit we follow Christ through the doors of death to the glorious presence of God our Father.

Reading

The Godward look is the secret of Christian hope . . . It is not simply a trembling, hesitant hope that perhaps the promises of God may be true. It is the confident expectation that they cannot be anything else but true.

William Barclay

Scriptures

For you, O LORD, are my hope,
    my trust, O LORD, from my youth.
Upon you I have leaned from my birth;
    it was you who took me from my mother's womb.
My praise is continually of you.
I have been like a portent to many,
    but you are my strong refuge.

My mouth is filled with your praise,
  and with your glory all day long.

Psalm 71.5–8

I pray that the God of our Lord Jesus Christ, the Father of glory, may give you a spirit of wisdom and revelation as you come to know him, so that, with the eyes of your heart enlightened, you may know what is the hope to which he has called you, what are the riches of his glorious inheritance among the saints, and what is the immeasurable greatness of his power for us who believe, according to the working of his great power. God put this power to work in Christ when he raised him from the dead and seated him at his right hand in the heavenly places, far above all rule and authority and power and dominion, and above every name that is named, not only in this age but also in the age to come.

Ephesians 1.17–21

Jesus said to his disciples, 'Do not let your hearts be troubled. Believe in God, believe also in me. In my Father's house there are many dwelling-places. If it were not so, would I have told you that I go to prepare a place for you? And if I go and pre-pare a place for you, I will come again and will take you to myself, so that where I am, there you may be also.'

John 14.1–3

Prayer

Father God, my strong refuge,
fill me with such a hope in your gracious promises
that my natural expectations are grounded
in the purposes of your kingdom,
and inspire me with your love.

By your Holy Spirit
seal my heart with the peace
which Jesus gives to those who follow him,
so that whatever happens to me,
I can rest in the assurance
that all things work together for good
for those who trust in you.

May I be prepared for opportunities
to respond with faith and love to your call
in whatever circumstances these might be.
Every day may my mouth be filled with your praise
and with your glory all day long.

Then I can look ahead in faith to all that is to come,
knowing that by the working of your great power
you are calling me to a glorious inheritance
with all your people through this life
and, in your mercy, into eternity.

11

Thankfulness

Reflections

I was intrigued years ago when I read J. B. Phillips' translation of the Beatitudes: 'How happy are the humble-minded, for the kingdom of heaven is theirs!' (Matthew 5.3). 'Happy', I thought: 'how can "happy" be the same as "blessed"?' It almost sounded irreverent. Later I noticed that Phillips' translation has been followed by the Good News Bible and other easy-to-read versions.

Eventually I learned there is biblical precedent for Phillips' choice of the word. In scripture, to be happy and to be blessed means virtually the same thing. A blessing is the authoritative pronouncement of a divine favour on a person. It is God smiling on us. The greatest blessing we have received is the coming of Jesus Christ as our Lord and Saviour. This was, and is, and ever will be, the highest of all gifts of God's grace and favour to us. Through this advent he has 'blessed us in Christ with every spiritual blessing' (Ephesians 1.3).

Our response to any gift is thanksgiving. The feeling of happiness which rises in us when we receive a gift from another person causes us to be thankful – and so we were taught from our earliest days the courtesy of expressing our gratitude. 'Remember to say thank you' is an admonition which is very familiar to most children brought up by conscientious parents.

Feelings of happiness are, of course, God's gift to us as his creatures. Times of happiness are inspired by the wonder of what it is to be human; they draw us together in a shared sense of thankfulness. We are happy when old friends whom we have not seen for a long time visit us, and we make it an occasion for celebration. When we wish someone a 'happy birthday' or a 'happy Christmas' we are not just saying we hope the celebration will be an enjoyable one for them; we are also conveying to them our gratitude for the joy they bring into our lives.

These experiences of human happiness can teach us how to be thankful for our experiences of divine favour which flow from knowing 'the breadth and length and height and depth' of the love of God (Ephesians 3.18). Because that love is immeasurably greater than any human love, so greater is our happiness and also our gratitude. It has often been said that, in the light of this truth, Christians should be the happiest people on earth.

I once knew a lady who seemed to me to overdo expressions of praise and thanksgiving to God. Working in an office and opening a letter which contained good news, or a cheque for a charity we were linked with, she would say out loud, 'Praise the Lord!' Struggling to discover how to operate a new piece of equipment, she would cry out, when she succeeded in making it do what she wanted it to do, 'Thank you, Father!'

At first, I thought it was rather amusing. But then my attitude changed when I realized that, as a devout Christian, this was her way of acknowledging the presence and grace of God in her life. She was doing what George Herbert prayed for: 'Teach me, my God and King, in all things thee to see; and what I do in anything to do it as for thee.' The rush of happiness she felt when she opened a letter or discovered a new skill caused her to lift her heart to the Lord in thanksgiving. She had learned the art of directing her happiness immediately towards God.

It can, of course, become a mere habit. But there is nothing wrong with a habit if it is a good one. It may be insensitive to cry aloud, 'Praise the Lord!' too frequently in the hearing of those who don't appreciate such expressions of devotion, but said inwardly it helps us to develop a mindset which encourages us to grow into a people for God's praise.

Occasions of human happiness, therefore, are crowned with God's grace when we thank him for them. This can extend to quite ordinary events. We receive some good news and we have a sudden feeling of joy: we offer an arrow prayer, 'Thank you, Lord, for . . .' We take part in something which makes us feel happy: as we leave, we praise God. Grace before and after meals is similar.

In this way the normal feeling of happiness is used as a vehicle with which to attach our thanksgiving to God, who is the source of all goodness and grace, and the experience becomes more than a feeling; it becomes a moment of spiritual rejoicing in the Lord.

In the Church's language of worship this kind of prayer is called 'a blessing'. Its roots go back to the prayers of Israel, when God's servants thanked him for blessings which they had received. Such was the prayer of Zechariah: 'Blessed be the Lord God of Israel, for he has looked favourably on his people and redeemed them. He has raised up a mighty saviour for us in the house of his servant David' (Luke 1.68–69). Such were the blessings Jesus said over the bread and the wine at the Last Supper.

The state of blessedness, therefore, is when we are conscious of receiving God's favour and when we respond to him with thanksgiving. It is the happiness of knowing that we are loved by God, and that he has given us the faculty in Christ to return that love in the Holy Spirit.

The great Christian festivals of Christmas, Easter, Ascension Day and Pentecost are celebrations to encourage us to praise and thank God as we journey on our spiritual pilgrimage through time. They come round in the cycle of the year to cheer us on; they give us opportunities of thanking God for the great saving events of the gospel, and what those events mean for us individually and as members of his people.

Corporate worship includes acts of praise which reach their crescendo in the celebration of the Lord's Supper. Its ancient title, the Eucharist, means 'the thanksgiving'. When, after the ministry of the Word, confession and intercession, the one presiding begins the Prayer of Thanksgiving, they call out: 'Lift up your hearts'. And we, the congregation, reply: 'We lift them to the Lord'.

It can be one of those moments when 'our hearts burn within us', and our feelings as well as our minds sing with thankfulness for Jesus yesterday, today, and for ever.

But then prayer continues with a recalling of the sacrifice of Christ which makes it possible to join in the Eucharist. That challenges us with an awesome thought: will we be able to sing with thanksgiving when, in following the victorious Lord, we are offered a crown of thorns?

Reading

Peter and the other disciples had seen the strong hands of God twist the crown of thorns into a crown of glory, and in hands as strong as that they knew themselves safe. They had misunderstood practically everything Christ had ever said to them, but no matter: the thing made sense at last, and the meaning was far beyond anything they had dreamed. They had expected a walk-over, and they beheld a victory; they had expected an early Messiah, and they beheld the Soul of Eternity. It had been said to them of old time, 'No man shall look upon my face and live'; but for them a means had been found. They had seen the face of the living God turned upon them; and it was the face of a suffering and rejoicing Man.

Dorothy L. Sayers

Scriptures

May God be gracious to us and bless us
  and make his face to shine upon us,
that your way may be known upon earth,
  your saving power among all nations.
Let the peoples praise you, O God;
  let all the peoples praise you . . .
May God continue to bless us;
  let all the ends of the earth revere him.

Psalms 67.1–3, 7

Let the peace of Christ rule in your hearts, to which indeed you were called in the one body. And be thankful. Let the word of Christ dwell in you richly; teach and admonish one another in all wisdom; and with gratitude in your hearts sing psalms, hymns, and spiritual songs to God. And whatever you do, in word or deed, do everything in the name of the Lord Jesus, giving thanks to God the Father through him.

Colossians 3.15–17

Jesus entered a certain village, where a woman named Martha welcomed him into her home. She had a sister named Mary, who sat at the Lord's feet and listened to what he was saying. But Martha was distracted by her many tasks; so she came to him and asked, 'Lord, do you not care that my sister has left me to do all the work by myself? Tell her then to help me.' But the Lord answered her, 'Martha, Martha, you are worried and distracted by many things; there is need of only one thing. Mary has chosen the better part, which will not be taken away from her.'

Luke 10.38–42

Prayer

Heavenly Father,
fill my heart with what I need most of all,
the word and peace of your Son, Jesus Christ;
then I can praise and thank you
for all the blessings I have received in my life.

I thank you for memories of people
whom I have loved
and who taught and encouraged me
as I sought to serve you.
Their faithful witness remains for me
models of discipleship patterned on those
who first followed your Son, Jesus.

I praise you for my family and friends
who surround me with your grace
and accept me for who I am,
forgiving my errors
and helping me to keep on the right path.

I thank you for blessing me with forgiveness
and renewing me in the Holy Spirit.

For the pains and difficulties I have experienced
and for all I learned of your power
to live through and beyond them.

I lift up my heart for all that lies ahead,
knowing that in the fellowship of your people,
you will uphold and guide me.
Help me to trust you for everything,
that the rest of my life will be filled
with thankfulness and praise.

12

Love

Reflections

'Love' is one of the most abused words in the English language. It can be used to describe a passing fancy ('I love geraniums'), an immoral act ('making love' outside marriage), or a casual greeting (as when a woman shop assistant calls her customer 'luv'). We distort its real meaning when we separate love and loving from the source of true love, God himself.

The emotion of love is universal. Yet it is much more than a feeling. The experience of beginning to love someone can be a marvellous first spark, but it is not the fullness of love. As love matures it engages the whole of ourselves. Everything about us is, as it were, caught up in it, and our abilities and hopes are enhanced by it. It is as if the desire for love, implanted in us by our Creator and suddenly released by the emotional reality, bursts out in fresh expressions of creativity. This happens in experiences of love – a man and a woman for one another, parents for a new baby, people who discover special friends. This happens not only to those with artistic skills but those with many other talents and visions.

Our ability to receive and express love begins from the moment we are born (or perhaps earlier, if some experts are to be believed). We learn what love means by experiencing it in our early years. Like the emergence of other emotions, that environment may be helpful or unhelpful in the maturing of love, according to the circumstances of our upbringing.

If our first experience of love is that of over-possessive or over-indulgent parents or guardians, then it is likely that, as we grow up, we shall have to struggle against self-centredness; we shall also have to learn that we need to offer love to others as well as receive it before we can know what love really is. If, on the other hand, our parents or guardians have been neglectful and uncaring, then our struggle is likely to be one of seeking love without really knowing what it is we are looking for, and without much idea of how to give and receive it.

Even those who have been brought up in what is recognized as a loving family still have much to learn. Because the need to love and be loved is so strong, there is always a danger of selfishness slipping into our affections and hopes. Feelings generated by sexual desire, family ties, common interests or the mysterious process whereby one personality is drawn towards another, can easily slip into self-indulgence. We 'love' the other person for what they can do for us, not for who they are.

Furthermore, the selfish element in our emotions can cause deceptions. Our memory, our desire or our imagination may idealize or fantasize the person we are attracted to. We become attached to the figure we want them to be rather than the person they really are. This is particularly the experience of young couples who marry and of friends who live together. We discover that the idealized picture of what the other was like has to be adjusted as we experience intimacy with the real person.

We discover, too, that love can be painful. The delight we experience in meeting and getting to know the one we love may be thwarted by disagreement or rejection. Jesus must have felt that pain when Peter denied that he knew Christ in the courtyard of the high priest (Matthew 26.69–75). The story of the disciple's betrayal is a parable of the truth that God can do everything except compel a man or woman to love him. We cannot do that, either.

Jesus said, 'You shall love your neighbour as yourself' (Matthew 19.19). He could not have anchored the love of our neighbour more securely than this. He might have said, 'You shall love your neighbour as you love God'. But that would have been less secure, for we can deceive ourselves about what loving God means; we can't deceive ourselves about what loving ourselves means!

When I was a parish priest, I was asked by a Belgian Jesuit I had met at an ecumenical gathering if I would let him live with me for a week and study the way I went about my pastoral duties. He was writing a thesis on the Church of England for a higher degree at Louvain University, and he wanted to learn something about its pastoral ministry first-hand.

He followed me like a shadow and came to everything – worship in church, daily prayers, a meeting of the parochial church council, confirmation classes, house groups, baptism preparation and visits to the sick. I don't know what he thought of it all, but he was obviously interested and asked me many questions after each event. What I found unnerving was being with parishioners and knowing that all the time he was assessing me and my relationship with them.

Looking back on that week, however, I see that it was an analogy of what we are seeking when we pray for God's grace in the relationships we have with other people, particularly those for whom we have feelings of warm affection or increasing love. We are trying to discern our emotions for others in the light of the love which God has for us and for them.

That means picturing all we know of the love of Jesus

Christ through the scriptures, through glimpses of that divine love we have seen in others, and through our own experience of his faithfulness. Then we ask the Father to send the Holy Spirit so that in our imagination we may picture Jesus with us and the other person, including those who are agnostic, atheist, or of other religions.

Hopefully this spiritual exercise will help us to understand ourselves better as we try to see our emotions as the Lord sees them. We ask the Lord to deliver us from false perceptions and selfish feelings, and to guide us in our relationships. We also bring the one we love into our intercessions and to seek the Spirit's guidance on the future.

And, if and when we experience the pain of loving – through rejection or disagreements – we should remember that the love that fails is still as much within the love of God as the love which is reciprocated. Love is measured by the spirit in which we feel it and offer it, not by its success or failure.

Reading

Only one act of pure love, unsullied by any taint of ulterior motive, has ever been performed in the history of the world, namely by the self-giving of God in Christ at the cross for undeserving sinners. Looking for a definition of love, we should not look in a dictionary, but at Calvary.

John Stott

Scriptures

I will bless the LORD at all times;
    his praise shall continually be in my mouth.
My soul makes its boast in the LORD;
    let the humble hear and be glad.
O magnify the LORD with me,
    and let us exalt his name together.
I sought the LORD, and he answered me,
    and delivered me from all my fears.

Psalm 34.1–4

Beloved, let us love one another, because love is from God; everyone who loves is born of God and knows God. Whoever does not love does not know God, for God is love. God's love was revealed among us in this way: God sent his only Son into the world so that we might live through him. In this is love, not that we loved God but that he loved us and sent his Son to be the atoning sacrifice for our sins. Beloved, since God loved us so much, we also ought to love one another.

1 John 4.7–11

When they had finished breakfast, Jesus said to Simon Peter, 'Simon son of John, do you love me more than these?' He said to him, 'Yes, Lord; you know that I love you.' Jesus said to him, 'Feed my lambs.' A second time he said to him, 'Simon son of John, do you love me?' He said to him, 'Yes, Lord; you know that I love you.' Jesus said to him, 'Tend my sheep.' He said to him the third time, 'Simon son of John, do you love me?' Peter felt hurt because he said to him the third time, 'Do you love me?' And he said to him, 'Lord, you know everything; you know that I love you.' Jesus said to him, 'Feed my sheep.'

John 21.15–17

Prayer

Take my heart, heavenly Father,
as I rejoice for the love you have shown me throughout my
    life,
a love that would not let me go.
And take with my heart my affections for others,
especially those whom I love very much.

I surrender my feelings for them to you as our Creator,
making us in your image
and implanting within us the ability
to love you and one another, as you love us.

I surrender my feelings for them to your Son, Jesus Christ,
who loves us and for that love
offered himself as a sacrifice for sin,
stretching out his arms on the cross
to embrace us and the whole world.

I surrender my feelings for them to your Holy Spirit,
by whose power you raised Jesus from the dead,
and through whom your love is poured out
on us and on all people everywhere.

Take my feelings and purge me
of anything unworthy of you.
Enable me to see those I love

as they really are in the light of your love for them,
and may they, too, be enabled to see me as I really am.

Above all, I ask that your will is fulfilled
in our relationship, however it develops,
and that our love for one another
may be within the love which flows from you,
Father, through the Son, and in the Holy Spirit.

Bibliography

Father Andrew, *The Life and Letters of Father Andrew S.D.C.*, edited by Kathleen E. Burne, A. R. Mowbray & Co., 1953.

William Barclay, *New Testament Words*, SCM Press, 1964.

Christopher Bryant, *Journey to the Centre*, Darton, Longman & Todd, 1987.

Ruth Fowke, *Coping with Crises*, Hodder & Stoughton, 1968.

John Macquarrie, *A Guide to the Sacraments*, SCM Press, 1997.

George A. Maloney, *Abiding in the Indwelling Trinity*, Paulist Press, 2004.

Ian Pettit OSB, *Your Sins Are Forgiven*, Darton, Longman & Todd, 1993.

Michael Ramsey, *Problems of Christian Belief*, quoted in Douglas Dales (ed.), *Glory Descending: Michael Ramsey and His Writings*, Canterbury Press, 2005.

Joyce Rupp, *Praying Our Goodbyes*, Inter Publishing Services, 1993.

Dorothy L. Sayers, *Creed or Chaos?* Methuen & Co. Ltd, 1947.

John Stott, *The Cross of Christ*, Inter Varsity Press, 1986.

William Temple, *Christianity and the Social Order*, Penguin Books, 1942.